When a Mother Follows Christ:

Laying the Foundation for Life

Katie Hoffman

Ano Klesis Publishing
Printed in the United States of America
1. Women's Issues. 2. Christian Living. 1. Title.

CONTENTS

INTRODUCTION

I'm very excited to be able to share this information with you. I know that whenever I am teaching mothers, I am getting to teach some of the most important people in the world! You are the women who are raising the next generation of adults, the people who will be here after we all have passed on. And I am so thankful to be able to give you the secrets to laying a strong foundation in your child's heart and character.

I get emails from women asking me about how they can solve different problems they are having with their children. I love helping women. But my heart always breaks when I get emails from women whose children are older and out of control. Not because it's too late for them (because it's not and God can do anything), but because so much time has already been lost.

In the world of saving money, the earlier you start, the greater your return. I found an interesting fact on the internet about money which explains my point:

"It REALLY pays to start now. Check this: if you save 100 bucks/month until you're 30 (for only 10 years, then you never save money again), and your… friend starts later–saving 100 bucks/month from age 30 to 65 (that's 35 years compared to your 10 years)–you will have way more money (over $100,000 more) than him at age 65. Start early and you will be rich." [1]

The point is that the earlier you start training character in your children, the more your investment will yield.

Again, let's say I decided to plant a garden. I buy my seeds in March, but I really don't have time to get out and start working in my garden until August. While I'm just starting to plant seeds, which may or may not grow because it's

[1](http://www.fortunewatch.com/you-dont-have-to-be-a-genius-to-get-rich/)

so late in the year, everyone else who planted early is reaping.

If you have young children, you can consider yourself abundantly blessed, because you still have *time*. The training and investing you put into your little children's lives now is a far better investment than anything you could ever do with the stock market or any 401K. What you invest in your children now is going to produce a greater return than what you invest into them when they are 30.

To help us remember what I'll be sharing throughout this book, I came up with an acronym. So the acronym is going to be SUPERCALIFRAGILISTICEXPEALIDOSHOUS. Did you get that? S-U-P-E-R-C-A-L-I... (I have a lot I want to talk about!) Okay, I'm kidding. *Following Christ as a mother* is about raising your children in such a way that they rise up and call you **BLESSED**, that God would be glorified. When the children of the Proverbs 31 women grow up, they call her blessed: "Her children rise up and call her BLESSED" (Proverbs 31:28). This book is organized into the acronym **BLESSED** to help you remember the core messages:

A godly Mom is one who trains **Behavior, Loves, Encourages, Safeguards, Sets** an **Example,** and **Disciplines**.

Behavior. Character is key.
Loves. Connect with your children so they desire to obey you from their heart.
Encourages. Teaches. Trains.
Safeguards. Protect your children from ungodly influences that would corrupt good morals.
Sets an Example. Gives her own behavior as a frame of reference for her children.
Disciplines. The importance of rules. Practical tips.

I want you to reap in your children the greatest yield possible! I want you to "have no greater joy that to hear that [your] children are walking in truth" (3 John 1:4). Blessed and biblical mothering means doing just what God says in His holy Word, so that our children rise up and call us blessed. Yes, beloved, it's an exciting and wonderful privilege we have!

CHAPTER ONE

Behavior

Consistent behaviors reveal character, and character is the key to child training. When it comes to training character, a lot of work is involved.

Character is defined as the inherent complex of attributes that determines a person's moral and ethical actions and reactions. In other words, character is who a person is, how they think, what they do, and what they believe. And when I talk about character, I am talking about godly character, character that is pleasing to God. Godly character is ultimately a genuine, fervent love for God manifested in a person's thoughts, actions, emotions, reactions, and behavior.

Let's look closely at 1 Cor. 13:4-7, and imagine all these attributes freely flowing out of your children.

> **1 Corinthians 13:4-7**
> "Love is patient and kind; love does not envy or boast; it is not arrogant or rude. It does not insist on its own way; it is not irritable or resentful; it does not rejoice at wrongdoing, but rejoices with the truth. Love bears all things, believes all things, hopes all things, endures all things."

In these verses we get a good picture of what godly character is like. If your children abound in these characteristics, I would definitely call you a blessed mother.

Additionally, at the end of this book is a resource titled, "Godly Character Traits". These are some of the attributes of godly character. You can use these sheets to teach your children what God requires of them.

THE IMPORTANCE OF CHARACTER

I believe character lays the foundation for the kind of relationships our children will have with others. Children with character will:

- -be better able to know what is right and what is wrong.
- -know how to obey the right authorities.
- -have an inner motivation to be kind to others.
- -respect you.
- -bring you joy as you grow older. "Discipline your son, and he will give you rest; he will give delight to your heart." Proverbs 29:17
- -be kind and respectful to their siblings.

Along with blessings you will reap now, there are some future blessings you can expect from your children also, if they possess godly character.

1. As adults, character will often help your children get better jobs, because they will be diligent, kind, hardworking, and truthful—companies want these types of employees.

2. It will make them hard workers at their jobs.

3. Their friendships will be deeper because they will genuinely care about others.

4. They will have an inner motivation to obey you as they get older because they will want to please God from their hearts.

5. They will be driven to perform well to please God.

6. They will not do shameful things as teenagers because they will a) have a strong conscience b) want to please God and c) be trained in the habit of doing what is right.

7. Godly character is part of pleasing and glorifying God, of living without wasting your life.

Now, here is the key: The more our children develop godly character, the less naturally they will be inclined to be rude and do things that provoke and sustain arguing, bickering, complaining, and fighting. If our children are raised to have godly character, sibling rivalry will be almost diminished. Godly character in our children is part of God's objective for us as mothers. And this book is written that we might raise children with godly character who will grow up to follow Christ, giving us rest and bringing delight to our hearts.

CHAPTER TWO

Love

As our children grow older, our ability to parent by authority decreases. If we have installed in our children a natural, healthy fear of consequences, we can parent well by authority when our children are young. We establish our authority by disciplining our children and teaching them to obey us. And our young children will mostly obey because of the authority we have over them.

But as our children grow older, we parent more and more by encouragement and influence.

The more we are connected to our children, the more we can encourage our children to do what is right. We can direct our children by our love, our words, and our prayers—if we first have that connected relationship with them.

This connection is CRUCIAL as they grow older. But we must begin nurturing that connection while our children are still young.

It's much **easier** to nurture a sweet, caring relationship with your child **now** while they are young than to turn the heart of a **rebellious, angry** teenager **back** to you once you have lost that connection. We can help avoid a future lack of relationship by spending time with our children now and showing love to them. When we are connected to our children:

1. They will want to know what we have to say.
2. They will want us to train them.
3. They will ask us to show them what is right and good.
4. They will be interested in hearing our advice and opinions.

Our discipline and our training will only be as effective as our level of connection with our children. We need to be connected to our children to have effective, heart-changing discipline.

Now is the time to get connected to your child. Here are four ways I have found that cause my children to bond with me.

1. **Smile**
Just by smiling often at your child, you can begin to win back a heart if you feel like you've begun already to lose it. I make it an aim of mine to smile every day as often as I can at both my husband and my children.

Back when my son Austin was about five years old, I realized I had begun to lose my connection with him. One of the significant things I noticed about that time was I had stopped smiling as much at him. I didn't realize I had gotten "meaner" and become more of a "woman of commands" until I realized one day that my son didn't really find much excitement in doing things with me. I became too "high pressure" and not filled with enough accepting, generous love.

Then I started making it a practice to smile at my son whenever I saw him or passed him during the day. I would smile at him when we sat down to eat together and when I greeted him in the morning.

And just by smiling, I began to see a great difference in his attitude toward me. He has always been trained to be very respectful, but he began to also "like" me. He began to seek me out more when he wanted to tell me something he was excited about. His heart became more tender toward me. My smile made me trustworthy in his young mind.

Every year our children either grow closer to us and more connected with us and influenced by us, or they grow more resistant to our parenting and hardened toward us. The less our children feel like we really love them, the less "impact" we will be able to have in our children's lives. The less you will be able to mother your child and help them become godly, responsible, caring adults.

We determine the state of the relationship we have with our children by how we treat and react toward them. If our hearts are tender toward our children, if we have opened up ourselves to them in love, then their openness toward us will grow.

2. **Listen**

When your child wants to talk, be ready to listen. **If you want an attentive child, be an attentive mom.**

When I was growing up, my dad had what he called a "Newspaper Policy." If he was reading the newspaper and one of us kids wanted to talk to him, he would tell us to come and hit the newspaper out of his hands. The point was to show us that we were always more important than the newspaper.

Imagine if one of us had the same policy with our kids? While you are reading an article on the internet, imagine if your child had your permission to come and turn off the computer. It would be a severe reminder of what is more important in life. (Hint: It's not the internet.)

I try to always be "available" to my kids, even when I have to do something. If I am working on a project, sorting laundry, cooking, answering an email, or whatever I am doing, if one of my kids comes to me because they have to tell me something, I make it a practice to stop everything I am doing, look them in the eyes, and listen to what they are saying.

Many mornings during breakfast, I'll sit down at the table with my children and ask, "Did you have any dreams last night?" I listen intently and care about what they have to say. My husband and I sometimes joke about the dream retelling. Our kids have taken enormous blocks of time retelling dreams. But it's good listening practice for me, and they really enjoy recounting their nighttime adventures.

3. **Be Affectionate.** Be tender with your children.

- Hug them every day.
- Kiss them every day.
- Tell them every day you love them—and to do these things all day long.
- Hold your children when they are sad.
- Cuddle with them when they go to bed or wake up.

You are the source of your children's physical needs. Make it a priority to give them physical, loving affection. Even teenagers need their moms to sit next to them on the couch, put their arms around them, and give them a prolonged hug. They especially need affection as they are entering a stage when many of their peers are seeking love from each other because they are <u>not</u> getting it at home.

4. **Above all, love your children.**
If you want to be connected to your children: Love your children, and make sure your children *know* how much you love them. You will establish a special connection that will allow

you to parent by influence as they get older because they will know their mother values them above her other hobbies and priorities.

Colossians 3:14 says, "And above all these put on love, which binds everything together in perfect harmony."

Let your children always see and know you love them dearly. Your love for your children needs to always be evident to them. If they see you as training their character without being motivated by your love for them, they will see it as a form of legalism -and they will resist you.

Let me say this again: If your children don't see <u>love</u> as your motivation for training their character, they will eventually <u>resist</u> you.

What does love look like?

True love has right priorities.

The other day my daughter came to me tattle-telling on her brother because he was not sharing the blanket with her. I was frustrated. "Why couldn't she deal with it herself? Is this really worth interrupting me over? Seriously, it's just a blanket. Play with something else." The problem was my focus was wrong when this was all happening. I was busy trying to finish something. I didn't want to be interrupted. I wanted to be able to concentrate on what I was doing. I had forgotten that my more important purpose in life is raising godly children.

When my priorities are right, it's amazing to me how much easier my kids are. That's because, instead of being a burden to me, they are *why* God has called me to be a mother. They are more important than my email or reading the news on the internet.

When I remembered that my children are far more important than whatever else I was doing, they became a blessing. And when I see them as a blessing and my purpose, I am able to gladly spend my day focused on training them.

If a mother has the attitude: "They are always arguing in the background. I can never concentrate because they are always interrupting me with a problem." –This is the problem. They are *in the background, an interruption, a problem.* How do you view your kids?? This is the question. Are they an interruption or the joy and delight of your day?

They pick up on how we feel about them. They must know you are training them because you really, deeply love them. And the blessing to you will include:

1. You will have greater closeness to your children as they grow up.
2. They will be nice to you and others.

Your kindness and sweetness (and firmness) toward your children is a crucial part of them wanting to know your God and wanting to serve Him. Your example can make or break your children's interest in following Christ. Their knowledge of God will be that He is sweet and kind to them, because their mother who loves God is sweet and kind toward them.

Pray daily to be a source of sweetness and kindness in your home. Write a note to yourself and place it somewhere you will see often, reminding you to pray daily for kindness toward your children.

Be very nice to your kids. Be careful to not show frustration with them when they go slow, don't understand what you are asking them to do, or want you to play with them all day long.

Instead:

1. Play with them.
2. Spend time everyday talking about the Bible to them.
3. Don't feel anxious when you are playing "boring" things with your kids, because the root of that feeling is the belief that you have something better, more exciting, more fulfilling, or more important to do.
4. Find joy and pleasure in knowing you are making such a difference in your children's entire lives. You are building their character.
5. Think of the "Cats in the Cradle" song—they're going to be just like you.
6. Talk sweetly to them.
7. Give them what they need.
8. Turn regular activities into fun family times. The last time I needed to cut the kid's toenails, I turned it into "spa day." I soaked each kid's feet in the foot bath, cut their nails, and gave hand massages. It was a special time for the kids and made routine grooming fun. I acted professional and put on a black apron. I gave

the kids each a special order drink while their feet soaked. And they loved the fun of it.

A woman who once struggled with kindness recounted the day when her attitude changed. She remembers clearly hearing the Scripture in her heart, "Your life is not your own" (1 Corinthians 6:19). It was if God spoke to her, "I want you to deny yourself and follow me, even if that means spending your whole day just playing with your kids." She obeyed her new conviction, even when it was really hard and she had to read the same boring book over and over again. But she said she's reaped everything she put it 100 fold, and now her sons are teenagers and she believes they are the godliest teenagers ever.

You may have heard it before, but quantity time IS quality time. In many cases, when a child has not deeply connected with his/her mom because the mom never took the time to spend hours with the child, as an adult the child will not have a large interest in pursuing much of a relationship with his/her mom.

I've seen this play out many times. The mom has her own interests, is emotionally preoccupied, and when the daughter or son grows up, he/she doesn't place a huge value on the relationship either. When the mom is confined to a convalescent home, and feels lonely and wishes for more visitors, the detached children dutifully pay visits, but they don't do it excitedly. They don't long for the times together. It's just an act of courtesy. And the mom is alone. It's "cats in the cradle" coming true. The kid will have learned from his/her own mother how to keep an emotional distance.

During these younger years when their mind, character, and personality are being formed, your children are extremely impressionable. They will notice what excites you, what makes you happy, what you worry about, how often you show thankfulness, and whether you think they are a burden or a blessing.

When you're at home, nobody knows how you are treating your kids. But people will see how you've treated your kids when you get out in public. Discerning folks will understand who you really are by how your children act. Of course, kids will be kids and they will have foolishness. But overall, do your children respect adults? Are they kind? Do they listen when people talk? Are they bossy? Remember, your children are reflecting you. Do you listen to your kids? Do you yell at them? Do you talk sweetly to them and smile? Do you make them feel important and wanted?

God says mothers are "to love their children". "Love is kind." "Love one another." (Titus 2:4; 1 Corinthians 13:4; John 13:34). This is part of your duty as a mother and a Christian. Not just to *feel* like you love your kids, but to make sure they know you love them. Obeying God always ultimately brings great happiness and satisfaction in your soul. If you feel depressed or empty, how much time have you spent playing with your kids today on their level? God has designed you to find fulfillment and joy in obeying Him. One of His commands is to love your children.

The conscience of a mother will be disturbed if she does not give her children the love and attention that she should. Her conscience will not be at rest if she is not fulfilling her duties as a mother; being kind, tender, and nurturing. She will lack peace and joy in her heart. ***Often a lack of joy and happiness is a sign of a disturbed conscience.*** You know you should be nicer to your kids. You know you should spend more time with them. Those things may not be exciting in the way the world advertises excitement, but those things will bring satisfaction to your soul. Your conscience will be at rest and you will begin to feel joy and gladness from the satisfaction of being a mother.

CHAPTER THREE

Encourage

A blessed mom encourages, teaches and communicates with her children. Give your child the gift of thorough, abundant communication.

Communication is vitally important as a parent. Teach your children about how to do the things you do. Explain why we add spices to foods. Teach them what you know and how to do it—whether you have knowledge with cooking, sewing, or hairstyling. Show them pictures of other countries and explain what life is like beyond what we are familiar with.

When you make a decision that affects them, tell them why you made the decision you made. If you decide to go to the bank to get money from the ATM, explain what a bank is and what the ATM machine is for. Teach your children about life.

Reassure your child that you are thrilled to be their mom. Let them know how much you value them. Talk to them of the great plan God has for their lives. Praise them when they try, even if they fail. Praise them when they *don't* get in trouble. Let your children know specific things that you like about them.

And, especially, teach them what it is that God requires of them.

Psalm 119:9-11 says: "How can a young man keep his way pure? By guarding it according to your word. With my whole heart I seek you; let me not wander from your commandments! I have stored up your word in my heart, that I might not sin against you."

Did you see the connection? Because God's Word had been stored up in David's heart, it helped keep him from sinning against God. As you teach your children what the Bible says, you are protecting them from sinning against God as they grow older.

Think about and consider: Do your children fear God and want to obey Him? Are they born again? If they are not born again, God's Holy Spirit will not be in them to enable them to obey. Ephesians 1:13 says, "In him you also, when you heard the word of truth, the gospel of your salvation, and believed in him, were sealed with the promised Holy Spirit." The Holy Spirit lives in every person who is a genuine Christian. And the Holy Spirit gives your children (and us) *the ability to obey.*

If your children are not genuine believers, they will lack the ability to obey from their hearts. Galatians 5:16-24 says,

"But I say, walk by the Spirit, and you will not gratify the desires of the flesh. For the desires of the flesh are against the Spirit, and the desires of the Spirit are against the flesh, for these are opposed to each other, to keep you from doing the things you want to do. But if you are led by the Spirit, you are not under the law. Now the works of the flesh are evident: sexual immorality, impurity, sensuality, idolatry, sorcery, enmity, strife, jealousy, fits of anger, rivalries, dissensions, divisions, envy, drunkenness, orgies, and things like these. I warn you, as I warned you before, that those who do such things will not inherit the kingdom of God. But the fruit of the Spirit is love, joy, peace, patience, kindness, goodness, faithfulness, gentleness, self-control; against such things there is no law. And those who belong to Christ Jesus have crucified the flesh with its passions and desires."

The sincere salvation of your children is necessary if they are going to have godly character.

LOVING YOUR CHILDREN BY WHAT YOU SAY TO THEM

Do you realize how much power you have to influence your children for the rest of their lives? The more you talk to your children, the more you are planting in their heads what they will believe as adults.

As a starting point for what exactly to focus on in your conversations with your children, determine your goals for your children and write them out. Write out the things you want them to know as adults. Not just "head knowledge", but morals, how you want them to approach life, what you want them to think about various issues, how you want them to treat others, and what they should know in this world.

This list could be longer. Think about what is important to you and determine to pass those values onto your children. This list will direct you in the decisions you make as a parent. It will help you know what to talk to your children about. You know, a child can grow into adulthood and never know things that the parents take for granted that the child will learn.

Sometimes parents just assume that because they think a certain way, the child will think that way too. This isn't always true. You must teach your child why you believe the way you do. You must teach them and train them how to do things.

I know a girl who had a mother who was quite organized. But she was not very organized. A friend finally came over to her house one day and taught her how to organize—how to sort similar things into categories, how to store those things together, etc. Her mother just figured she would learn how to organize. But she didn't. Not everything comes naturally to everyone. She needed to be trained. (And I'll tell you a secret... that girl is me!)

But my parents did a wonderful job of raising me as a Christian. My mom set an example for me of a woman who prays. My dad faithfully helped me memorize Bible verses as I was growing up. They took me to church every week.

Those things I learned have not left me, and I am very appreciative toward my parents for not neglecting to teach me about God and bringing me to salvation through Jesus Christ.

Teaching your children and bringing them to faith in Christ, like my parents did, is the most important thing they will ever learn. If they go their whole lives being "good people" but they never believe on Jesus as their Lord and Savior, they will have missed the whole point of life.

They need to know that good works are not enough to enter heaven. A good place to start is the Ten Commandments. Go through each of the Ten Commandments with your children and ask them specifically if they have broken any of the commandments. (They can be found in Exodus 20).

Even by age 3, each of my children had lied to me at least once. Next, you can ask your children if they think they will be innocent or guilty on Judgment Day of breaking God's rules. Since we've all broken at least one of the Ten Commandments, we will all be guilty. James 2:10 says "For whoever keeps the whole law and yet stumbles at just one point is guilty of breaking all of it."

Next, tell them what will happen on Judgment Day. Tell them so their hearts are ready to receive the good news of Jesus with great joy. Revelation 21:8 says very clearly what happens to everyone who breaks God's rules. "But as for the cowardly, the faithless, the detestable, as for murderers, the sexually immoral, sorcerers, idolaters, and all liars, their portion will be in the lake that burns with fire and sulfur, which is the second death."

Usually the heart and conscience of a little child is so tender, that by the time you get to this point they are more than ready to hear about Jesus.

But I teach my children *why* Jesus had to die on the cross, which is because we have broken God's rules, and because we will be judged as guilty by God for our sin, because this is an essential part of the gospel. And one of my personal goals for my kids is for them to understand the gospel.

Jesus saves us from the punishment we would have if we were left alone in our sins. Teaching my children about the great sacrifice Jesus made for their sins helps them understand how much God loves them. I explain that when Jesus died on the cross, our sins were nailed to that cross with Jesus. God's anger toward our sin was satisfied in Jesus. Our guilt is removed when we believe on Jesus.

And then I explain the glorious resurrection. Three days after Jesus was crucified on a cross, He rose from the dead and became alive again. The salvation of your children is the most glorious goal you can ever have for them. And you can always include telling them that this is why we celebrate Easter.

This last year at Christmastime I taught my son that Christmas is the celebration of Jesus' Birthday, as I try to do every year. We were driving home from the store at night a few weeks before Christmas and my son Austin was looking at the houses with lights. As we passed a house that was really decked out, and just covered with lights and decorations, Austin said, "Those people must really love God." I said, "What do you mean?" He answered, "Look at how hard they worked decorating for Jesus' birthday!"

Remember: Establish what you want your children to know by making a list of your goals for them. The more you teach your children what is true, the more you protect them from believing what is not true.

CHAPTER FOUR

Safeguard

Studies have been done on children and adolescents to figure out whether peer influence or parental influence is more powerful. The conclusion is that, overall, by the time children are teenagers, peer influence is stronger than parental influence.

And I have talked with a lot of moms who have seen what a difference peer influence can make. I met a lady who had a 7 seven year old daughter with severe ADHD. The lady was wonderfully sweet, and this was her only child. She was a single mother who had to work full time. But during Christmas break, the mother didn't have to work and she was able to be home with the daughter each day. During that time, the daughter seemed to do much better. By the end of Christmas break the daughter was noticeably more respectful, polite, and attentive toward her mom.

But when she came home after just the first day of school, her attitude had kicked right back into full gear. She started back-talking to her mom again. Just one day of peer influence changed her that drastically.

This is what the Bible also asserts. Proverbs 13:20 says, "Whoever walks with the wise becomes wise, but the companion of fools will suffer harm." In the KJV this says, "A companion of fools shall be destroyed." The New Living Translation says, "Whoever walks with fools will suffer harm."

This seven year old daughter had suffered harm by her exposure to other kids who were unwise. She had picked up the disrespect of those kids who were disrespectful around her.

Understanding this verse has changed my approach to parenting! This is another one of those things I talked about at the beginning that has really changed my life and given me vision for raising my kids.

The Bible also describes a specfic group of people who are more likely to be foolish. Proverbs 22:15 says "*Folly* is bound up in the heart *of a child*, but the rod of discipline drives it far from him." Children have foolishness bound up in their hearts.

Undisciplined kids are going to be foolish—because it is the rod of correction that makes kids wise. And if you're not carefully safeguarding your kids, undisciplined kids can potentially become the foolish *companions* of your children.

Which means, we need to protect our children from harmful influences, which includes **unsafe situations, untrustworthy people, and even kids their own age sometimes when they are bad influences.**

Safeguards are necessary for those times when your children need you to watch out for them. If an eleven year old boy was put in a peer environment, with all the kids his age doing something he wasn't allowed to do, it would only be a matter of time before the pressure would become almost unbearable. So instead of putting your children in high pressure situations, where they have to resist heavy peer influence just to obey you, it is usually better to just protect them from those types of things until they are old enough or strong enough in character to easily resist.

Ungodly influences are a powerful force that can weaken our impact as parents. They can potentially undo part of the character we have worked so hard to create in our children. The more junk that goes into our children's hearts, the less influence we will be able to have with our children. The "junk" is the harmful influences in our children's lives.

Even though I *wanted* to be naughty as a teenager, practically every bad thing I did as a teenager could have been **prevented** by my parents if I had no one to do those bad things with. It's definitely something to remember as your children grow older.

As mothers, you are in the greatest position of any one to **safeguard** your children from harmful influences. That is why it is so important now to connect with your child and safeguard them from negative peer influence. I'm not for total isolation of kids or anything like that. But I do think it is wise to protect your children from kids who will negatively influence them, especially because those influences are so powerful.

CHAPTER FIVE

Set an Example

This is one of the things I am most excited about telling you as a mom, because this one thing has made a HUGE difference in our house.

Let me share with you what I have learned and seen firsthand from experience. At around 6 years of age, my oldest son began to get easily frustrated with his younger sister and talk to her disrespectfully. At first, I couldn't understand what was going on. I was consistently disciplining every time he was disrespectful or whiny, and I thoroughly taught him that these behaviors are never allowed. Yet I still dealt with these things on a daily basis.

Yet even with my diligence in discipline, these character flaws were still uncontrolled. It wasn't until I changed one thing in my parenting that I saw a HUGE, almost night and day difference.

And here is the secret: Your children, whether we like it or not, will be, to some degree, a reflection of you. I realized I was acting snappy. I was demonstrating to my kids how to act. If you are a mother who is always respectful and loving to your husband, your children will see a real life example and learn from that example how to be loving and respectful to each other and you. It is very hard for us as humans to behave in a way that has never been modeled for us. (I am talking about good behaviors, not naturally bad behaviors.)

If I asked you to stand up right now and walk like a runway model—and you agreed to do it—what would come to mind? If you've never walked a runway before, you would most likely try to visualize a time when you saw someone walk a runway, on TV or wherever you saw it. Then you would try and walk like you remember them walking. If you have never seen someone walk a runway, this would be much harder. You wouldn't have a frame of reference for ***how*** to walk like a model.

We are like that as humans. We learn how to do things by watching other people do them. We all learn from each other. And our children are a prime example of this. They learn their positive behaviors from the people they observe and admire.

And with children, things need to be repeated—A LOT. Often without even realizing it, our actions are repeated for our children constantly. We repeat our actions every day, though we may not verbally remind our children how to behave every day. And this can really work in your favor, if you are respectful, cheerful, and polite toward your husband in front of them.

Your children are going to learn how to be respectful, loving, thankful, and considerate by watching you. And specifically, they are going to learn those things by how you treat your husband and how you treat them. This is the primary frame of reference they will have. You set the example for your children. They will model their behavior after your behavior.

Once I realized what the problem was, I made a list to fix it.

TACKY YELLOW NOTEBOOK PAPER

I wrote out the changes I needed to make on a yellow piece of notebook paper and taped it to the front of my kitchen cupboard. Yes, I know this is tacky—but sometimes we need tacky, right? If what the paper says is something I need to be reminded of often, a beautiful framed picture with small wording at the bottom isn't always going to cut it. So I taped the tacky piece of yellow paper to my cupboard so I could see the words written on it every day. And these are the words I believe are so important that I needed this ugly reminder.

The Paper is called "**<u>Character Goals</u>**". Remember, in some cases, more is caught than taught. With impulsive behavioral responses to situations, I believe this is often the case. Our children do as we do, not as we say. That is why I believe it is important we behave in the same way we expect our children to behave.

So here is my list—verbatim:

1. I want Austin to be <u>patient</u> with people when they make mistakes, so I must be <u>patient</u> with Austin when he makes mistakes.

2. I want Austin to be a good listener, so I must be a good listener to Austin.
3. I want Austin to always talk in a respectful voice, so I must talk in a respectful, non-annoyed voice at all times with Austin.
4. I want Austin to pay close attention when I talk to him, so I will pay close attention when Austin talks to me.
5. I want Austin to give a gentle answer even when he is frustrated, so I will answer Austin with a gentle voice even when I am frustrated.

Because sometimes it's easy as a mom to get annoyed at our kids FOR JUST BEING KIDS. "Why did you bump into your sister as she was walking to the table? Now milk has spilled out of her cereal bowl? Why weren't you paying attention? Look out next time!" Right? Have you ever done this?

Or while you're deep in thought answering an email and you hear your kids saying the same thing 10 times, "Mom, mom, mom, mom, mom, mom, MOM!" And then when our child is absorbed in what they are doing, we say, "I want your room to be clean by the time daddy comes home from work. *Did you hear me? What did I just say then*?"

And we are SURPRISED that our child didn't drop everything to pay attention to what we said.

You set the example for your children. They will model their behavior after your behavior, whether it is frustration, thankfulness, respect for others, etc. If you are respectful toward your husband, they will learn to be respectful toward you. If you get angry with your husband when you don't get your way, they will learn to throw a fit when they don't get their way. If you model anxiety and frustration as a way of life, your children will learn how to be whiny, irritable, and high-strung also.

My point is this: we must *set the example* for our kids so they will learn how to behave.

THE WALMART WOMAN

I saw a woman in Wal-Mart with two kids who kept fighting in the basket. The kids kept arguing, grabbing at toys, and yelling at each other. The mother kept turning toward the kids and screeching, in the same tone of voice the kids were using with each other, "Stop it! Stop it! Stop taking that toy. Stop your fighting!" A minute later the kids were at it again. And all ten minutes we were in the same aisle, it kept happening. (It was a major clearance sale aisle.)

I can guess the mother was just exhausted, as this scenario probably happens in her house all day long. Her husband probably doesn't like coming home from work. She probably doesn't like being home either. But she is feeding her problem, and it keeps getting bigger.

Do your kids have an example of how to fight with each other from you? To avoid this—never argue with your husband in front of your kids. **Let your children learn respect and obedience *from your example***.

Model for your children how to talk nice, how to get along with others, how to not be demanding, how to be patient with others by the way you treat them and by the way you treat their daddy.

When your children see you react to a situation in a sinful way, you're setting an example for them. If they model your example, the foolishness and bad habits that result may last their entire lives.

A godly example will correct this. Saying sorry and admitting what you have done wrong, even for past mistakes, will help teach your children what is right and what is wrong.

FOLLOWING CHRIST IN FRONT OF YOUR CHILDREN

Just as you set the example in how you act around the house, you set a huge example in spiritual things also.

I clearly remember my mom and her friend on their faces praying in the living room. As a child, I didn't quite understand the significance of that prayer time. But when I became an adult, what is something I love to do? Pray on my face with my friends!

I also remember as a child when my dad was part of a prison ministry. He went to the prison to share his faith with a group of men from our church. During his time there, a man who he personally talked to committed his life to Christ. My dad was ecstatic! When he came home, I could see the great joy overflowing from him as a result of his experience! Seeing that example of my dad caused me to also desire to have the joy of watching a person be converted. From my dad's example, I saw telling others about Jesus as an awesome, joy-filled experience.

Don't ever let having children be an excuse for not preaching the gospel. Yes, it may be much, much harder to carry on a conversation while bouncing a baby on your hip, occupying your three year old and keeping an eye on your six year old, but it will one day be worth it. Even if you never see a soul become converted, the seeds you are planting in your children can produce priceless fruit!

That doesn't mean you have to stop everything you're doing every time you meet an unbeliever, but if God opens the door to talk about Him to someone, it may be one of your greatest training moments as a mom. Because when we tell others about Jesus in front of our children, we are giving them a practical example of how to live for Christ in this world.

It's always a special moment when God gives us joy and pleasure from seeing the difference we are making in our children's lives. Last week we were leaving for the zoo when I called upstairs, "Austin, where are you? Why aren't you ready to go?" A minute or two later, Austin appeared. Out the door and to the zoo we went.

When we got there, Austin took some gospel tracts out of his pocket and said, "I brought tracts to pass out. That's what I was doing upstairs when you were waiting for me." Austin blessed me by his sincere desire to see people won to Christ. I want children of deep conviction and character, and I praise God for allowing me to see that character already being formed in their hearts.

Children who talk about Jesus to others, now and as adults—their hearts are more sealed and inclined to grow up following God, if they have tasted the great joy that comes with preaching the gospel. If they have eaten the sweet fruit of sharing their faith, that is what they will hunger for. If they have never enjoyed the joy that comes from witnessing, they may never have a desire for following Christ in that way.

Imagine the impact you will have on your children when you openly share your faith in Christ with others in their presence! Their hearts will be forever sculpted by seeing the joy you find in following Christ. They will know from their own experience that more joy and satisfaction comes from following Christ than from following the world. They will have seen your joy over telling people about Jesus, and it will create in them an appetite for that satisfaction. If your children grow up preaching the gospel as a part of their lives, think what sort of insurance that is against backsliding as a teenager! I'm not saying they still can't backslide, but if they can taste the joy found in Christ as children, they will forever long for it. I know that was definitely the case with me!

CHAPTER SIX

Discipline

Rules make life easier. When you have established, consistently enforced rules, your children know exactly what you want and expect from them. And when they follow the rules, life is happy and peaceful. Discipline comes in when children disobey those rules. Discipline is how your children learn the importance of the rules, and find the motivation to obey at all times.

Once rules are established, you don't have to keep telling your kids what you want from them. They already know because you've made it clear by establishing consistent rules.

Now, before I go on, let me explain the difference between God's rules and my personal rules. God's rules are non-negotiable for every household and every family. His rules never change and must always be obeyed.

God's rules include:

1. All the character traits on the "Godly Character Traits" resource. His rules also include avoiding the sins on the "Sinful Behaviors" resource. This is not a comprehensive list—just some of the more common sins that children are likely to commit.
2. They include the Ten Commandments: do not steal, do not use God's name in a way that does not show respect, honor your parents, do not give a false testimony against someone, and all the other commandments from Exodus 20.
3. And for children, they include Ephesians 6:1, which says, "Children, obey your parents in the Lord, for this is right.

OUR PERSONAL HOUSEHOLD RULES

We also have personal rules for our house. These rules will very likely be different for each family. Some of these rules will change as our kids get older. So with that said, here they are:

1. **Do your morning routine everyday as soon as you wake up.** Now that my kids are ages 3, 6, and 9, they all have a morning routine they are supposed to do. Some of these things include getting dressed, brushing their teeth, and making their bed. And then they each have additional jobs that are related to their ages.

2. **Do not touch things that are not yours unless you ask first.** Having this rule in place really helps when we are out at someone else's house, at church, and at the store.

3. **Always say, "Please, Thank You, and You're Welcome."**

4. **Do what we (Daddy and Mommy) say the first time.** As soon as we ask our children to do something, they need to say, "Yes, Daddy" or "Yes, Mommy" and start doing it. Only after that can they state their case (if they must) and say, "May I please ____."

5. **No murmuring, complaining, or discontentment is allowed. Give thanks in everything with a smile.** The Bible says that

complaining is sin. It also says to give thanks in everything. Learning this habit as a child is the best time.

6. **When mommy or daddy calls you, answer and come immediately.**

7. **When somebody is talking to you, look at them (at their face) and do not interrupt.**

8. **When you want to tell somebody something, go find them first and then tell them. No yelling.**

10. **Never grab something out of someone else's hand (unless it is something dangerous.)**

11. **No standing or jumping on furniture.** This especially helps us avoid problems when we are at other people's houses or at church.

12. **Always talk in a respectful voice and say respectful words.** An example of *not* doing this would be if my son said harshly, "Tyla, come here!" He would be talking rudely

to her and not respectfully. In this case, the tone of voice is very important.

13. **When you ask somebody a question or say something to them, do not keep saying it over and over again. Wait for them to answer. Wait at least 20 seconds**. You know sometimes when you're loading the dishwasher or doing something and you are just deep in thought and your kids say, "Mommy, Mommy, can I watch a movie?" and you don't hear them right away, so they keep asking over and over again. But if they would just wait a minute you would be able to think about what they asked and give them an answer. So after my kids ask a question, they need to count to 20, or at least wait a few moments before saying anything else, so I can process my thoughts.

I do have to review the rules with them, because it's amazing how quickly kids can forget rules.

Once you have determined your personal household rules, when your children disobey, you can show them the rule they have broken, or the Bible verse that describes what they have done wrong.

If you have one sibling who takes advantage of the others, or is rude in the way he/she talks to the others, and he/she gets away with it, it will create resentment, bitterness, and erode character in *both* children. Our job as mothers is to train and correct behavior.

Consider fighting, arguing, selfishness, rudeness, yelling, impatience, complaining, bitterness, remembering wrongs, and talking in a rude voice—consider these things as offences that need discipline and correction. The attitudes of your children on the inside can be just as wrong as outward disobedience.

Consistent discipline helps to train character. You may have to start by disciplining 20 times a day when you're focused on training character. But you can tell yourself, "Well I may have to do that for the first couple days, but as I discipline, I am training character. And as they learn character, I will go from disciplining 20 times a day to a few times a day to rarely ever."

If you discipline consistently, you will notice that you will have to discipline ***much less*** than the mother who disciplines inconsistently.

Discipline your children for their good and their benefit. I think that often we become frustrated with our children when they are out of control. We can train and teach our children to be delightful and obedient, so we can enjoy our children for the blessings they are.

You can never have too much love for your children. But true love includes training, correcting, and disciplining. **Love** your child though discipline.

Proverbs 13:24 says, "Whoever spares the rod hates his son, but he who loves him is diligent to discipline him." If you do not teach your children how to obey rules, it is a sign of hatred, not love.

Proverbs 29:15 says, "The rod and reproof give wisdom, but a child left to himself brings *shame to his mother*." This verse is important because it talks about the two parts of discipline. The rod and the reproof. Reproof is talking to our children and making sure they understand what they did wrong and how they can behave correctly next time. This communication and training is vital. And the rod refers to what we usually call a spanking. This is NOT talking about child abuse. I am not talking about injuring your children. A rod would be like a wooden kitchen spoon around 18 inches long which stings the bottom.

Something that only stings, not injures. And this is done ONLY for the child's good and for their benefit—not to release your anger.

When you discipline your children, you are teaching them a very valuable message, and it is this: There are painful consequences to bad behavior. You are teaching them that it hurts to disobey. You are showing them how *serious* sin really is.

And remember the last part of the verse? The thought of being overcome with shame as you get older is terrifying! Yet we can all think of children who are now older and who are bringing shame to their mothers! But the Bible tells us how to prevent this:

Proverbs 29:17 "Discipline your son, and he will give you rest; he will give <u>delight</u> to your heart." ***Delight***—Oooh!!

How do we gain this? The rod and reproof, and by staying with our children—not leaving them to themselves. Remember: a child left to himself brings shame to his mother. But if you discipline them, they will give *delight* to your heart. We don't let them "learn for themselves" when they are still young. We *train* them.

Here are some tips for disciplining:

- Don't speak in a different voice than your normal tone—teach them to pay attention when you are talking, not just when you are yelling. Otherwise, they will think that you only say the important stuff when you are yelling.
- When you ask or tell them to do something, get their full attention, talk directly to your children, and say it clearly one time.
- Before you go somewhere with your children, tell them exactly how you want them to behave and tell them what the exact rules will be.
- Before you go somewhere, pray with your children and let them pray to ask God for obedient hearts.

Practical Things

Here are eleven practical tips to solve everyday problems:

1. **Teach your children to use their words—to talk instead of grabbing, fighting, and pouting.**

I make my children use their words when they need something from each other. The other day I asked my kids, "Would you rather walk to the park or walk to Chicken Express and have lunch?" Austin said, "Chicken Express" and Tyla said, "the park". So I told Austin, "Okay Austin. We are not going to both places. You need to get Tyla to pick Chicken Express if we are going to go there." I say that because I know he will have to practice and develop his skills of communication and persuasion. Those skills will be especially necessary as our children seek good jobs and seek other important things in life.

So my son says to his sister, "If we go to Chicken Express we can eat yummy chicken. It will be so fun. Think about how good the chicken will taste. Don't you want to go to Chicken Express?" And so he has won his sister over to his side. No fighting. No arguing. Just peaceful, sweet, effective communication.

2. **Resolve disagreements by getting slightly involved.**

I've seen some secular parenting magazines and other sources talk about sibling fighting and say, "Don't get involved." But I think it's wise to get involved. Proverbs 29:15 says, "The rod and reproof give wisdom, but a child left to himself brings shame to his mother."

Do get involved. But you don't necessarily have to solve the problem. This is how I get involved: I tell my kids, "If I hear fighting, you're BOTH getting in trouble." And then I tell them: "The Bible says, 'A harsh word stirs up anger, but a soft answer turns away anger" (Proverbs 15:1).

It may be that one kid is provoking the other child to get them in trouble. If one of the children is being very kind to the other, firm but kind, that child will usually be able to avoid conflicts for both. And it solves the problem of one kid trying to get the other child in trouble or provoking the other child for whatever reason. If they know they are both getting in trouble, they will try to *avoid* provoking their sibling.

3. Have them take turns.

When they both want to play with something, I say, "Let (one of the kids) play with it for 2 minutes and then it's your turn to play with it for two minutes." Then I set the timer and monitor them to make sure they are switching back and forth.

4. Assign playtimes to older siblings.

When the younger sibling wants the older sibling's time and the older sibling wants to play alone, I will assign my oldest times when he is to play with his sister or brother. I'll say, "You can play by yourself right now, but in 20 minutes I want you to play with your sister."

5. Provide activities for your children.

As I've said before, occupy your children's time so they are too busy to fight. Keep the kids busy in routine activities (Morning routine, school, helping around the house) and make playing together a ***privilege***. Our rule is that our kids can either play together nicely or they help with the work.

6. Arm your children with the right attitudes.

One example of this is: My husband has repeatedly told our oldest son, "Your job is to protect your sister and brother." Because of this, he knows protecting his sister and brother is his job and he takes it very seriously. He watches out for them and helps us so we haven't yet had any serious injuries.

Your children will often act and react based on the information you have given them. Make sure they always understand what it is you want from them. And if it is something they may not understand easily, show them by your example. For instance, when you tell them to "give thanks in all circumstances", also demonstrate thankfulness yourself in difficult times so they can see practically what it means to be thankful even when they don't get what they want.

7. Praise your children.

Whenever your children do what is right and good, point it out and let them know. You will be teaching them what right behavior is. By praising them, they learn what to do again. So tell them what a great job they are doing of being kind when they play well together. Praise them for sharing and for considering one another more highly than themselves.

8. Discipline for fighting and arguing.

When you catch your children fighting or arguing, in most cases you will need to discipline both of them even if it seems to be just one of their faults. Why? Because "a soft answer turns away wrath."

If one of the siblings is truly and completely innocent, having done nothing to provoke the other, and having responded to the other sibling's sin with all gentleness, you probably wouldn't have known there was a fight at all. Plus, when your children know it will be a general rule that they will both be disciplined for fighting, there is no motivation to provoke the other sibling to get in trouble, since they know they will get in trouble too.

If you are consistent with this, it will soon make sense to them and sibling problems will quickly vanish.

9. Always be consistent.

I had the opportunity to observe Ruth one day as she was home with her kids. The scenario went something like this: The child was in a habit of fit throwing. And if the child wanted something, the mother would repeatedly give in. Now, this was not a baby or even a toddler we are talking about, but a school aged child. If the child wanted a toy or a food or drink item, and the child threw a fit, the mother would give it to her child to keep him happy instead of teaching her child to share.

However, she knew something wasn't right, so she would threaten to spank the child if he threw a fit again. But instead of spanking, she gave in 80% of the time! She kept threatening and rarely disciplining, and when she did discipline it was so minor and the comfort so great—there was no reason for the child to obey.

When the older sibling was kicking the younger sibling, the response was, "Stop that. Stop that." And that was it! Well the child, of course, didn't listen or care. So he kept on kicking. Finally the mom got up from her chair and the child stopped kicking. Once the mom sat down, the kicking started up again. So the mom stands up as if she was going to discipline, and the kicking stopped. So the mom sat back down. And this happened over... and over... and over...

Here is a good rule to follow that I learned from a wise mother of 5, who herself grew up in a very godly home: If your children are doing something naughty, and you ask them to stop and they disobey, but then they do obey when they see you moving in the direction of disciplining them—you need to discipline them.

When they move AFTER they see that they are going to be punished, they are learning to obey through THREAT. They are not being obedient for obedience sake, or because they were told to obey. They are learning to only obey ONCE they see you coming, and not a second sooner. Of course, they will occasionally obey at other times when they feel like it or to keep you from catching on, but they know. They are smart. They know that they don't have to obey immediately and it will still be okay for them.

In some cases, the reason a mother doesn't discipline is that she wants acceptance from her child. She would be disturbed if her child was mad or upset with her. This ungodly "fear" of her child's rejection can ruin a child. If a mother is consistent with discipline, and stops threatening completely, her child will be a lot happier with her in the long run.

The sad end of this kind of parenting is often deep seated rebellion when the children grow up. The children have never learned how to be respectful, and so as teenagers, they walk all over their mothers, while the mothers sit home and weep and wonder, "What happened? I tried so hard to love my child. How did he/she become so rebellious and disrespectful?" The answer is that the child has been raised all his life to be selfish and disrespectful. There were really no surprises.

10. Don't make excuses for sin.

Another example is the mother who always has an excuse for the child's sin. When her child talks rudely to her friends, the mother will quickly explain: "She is tired. She is hungry." Or even, "I know it's not an excuse, but she really is tired." Now, of course sometimes children are very tired and it does affect their behavior. I think it can drastically affect their behavior.

But remember, we are training character. So we can't say to our children, "Well I know you're tired so I will let you hit your friends and yell at them and call them bad names because you're just tired." Because when they are teenagers we don't want them to say, "But mom, I stole the candy because I was hungry. I yelled at you and called you bad words because I was tired." Sin is still sin even when we are tired. Tiredness can really bring out our sinful nature. But we still have to teach our children how serious and wrong sin is.

11. Teach them to consider others.

When my kids are playing with other kids, and they both want something, I always tell my children to give the toy to the other kids. This teaches them the practical application of what the Bible says, "In humility count others more significant than yourselves" (Philippians 2:3 ESV).

If my children have friends over and they begin to fight over a toy, sometimes I will make them give the toy to the kids—to keep. The principle I am trying to instill in my children is that "people are more important than things". My children's character is a million times more valuable than any toy they will ever own. As mothers, you are training character. That is your goal and your job.

IN CONCLUSION

"Train up a child in the way he should go; even when he is old he will not depart from it" (Proverbs 22:6). Without character training, you haven't trained up a child in the way he should go.

Loving your child means you discipline them appropriately for their good. **Love includes discipline.** Proverbs 17:25 says, "A foolish son is a grief to his father and ***bitterness*** to her who bore him." Foolish children will bring bitterness. Foolish children will cause us great frustration.

And the Bible gives us a specific way to keep our children from growing up to be foolish. The solution is found in Proverbs 22:15, which says, "Folly is bound up in the heart of a child, but the rod of discipline drives it far from him." **Discipline *removes* foolishness**.

Here is the key: If we want to be mothers whose children grow up and call us blessed, it starts with the example we set in our marriages, and the way we mother them in the home. The rules, the discipline, the love, and the protection we provide will guide their character and shape them into the adults they will soon become.

RESOURCE 1

Godly Character Traits

Love—

- "See to it that you really do love each other intensely with all your hearts." 1 Peter 1:22
- "And above all things have fervent love for one another." 1 Peter 4:8

Kindness—

- "Put on then, as God's chosen ones, holy and beloved, compassion, kindness, humility, meekness, and patience." Colossians 3:12
- "Be kind to one another, tenderhearted." Ephesians 4:32

Humility—

- "Clothe yourselves, all of you, with humility toward one another, for 'God opposes the proud but gives grace to the humble.'" 1 Peter 5:5

- "All these things my hand has made, and so all these things came to be, declares the Lord. But this is the one to whom I will look: he who is humble and contrite in spirit and trembles at my word." Isaiah 66:2

Diligence—

- "Whatever you do, work heartily, as for the Lord and not for men." Colossians 3:23
- "Whatever your hand finds to do, do it with your might." Ecclesiastes 9:10

Paying Attention—

- "So then, my beloved brethren, let every man be swift to hear, slow to speak, slow to wrath." James 1:19

Respect for others—

- "Honor everyone." 1 Peter 2:17
- "Outdo one another in showing honor." Romans 12:10

Wisdom—

- "The beginning of wisdom is this: Get wisdom, and whatever you get, get insight." Proverbs 4:7
- "The fear of the Lord is the beginning of wisdom." Psalm 111:10

Honesty—

- "Do not lie to one another." Colossians 3:9
- "Let the thief no longer steal, but rather let him labor, doing honest work with his own hands, so that he may have something to share with anyone in need." Ephesians 4:28

Thoughtfulness—

- "And let us consider how to stir up one another to love and good works." Hebrews 10:24
- "Let each of you look not only to his own interests, but also to the interests of others." Philippians 2:4

Patience—

- "Be patient with each other, making allowance for each other's faults because of your love." Ephesians 4:2

Forgiveness—

- "Love is not irritable, and it keeps no record of when it has been wronged." 1 Corinthians 13:5
- "Be kind to one another, tenderhearted, forgiving one another, as God in Christ forgave you." Ephesians 4:32

RESOURCE 2

Sinful Behaviors

Selfishness—

- "Love does not demand its own way." 1 Corinthians 13:5
- "Let no one seek his own good, but the good of his neighbor." 1 Corinthians 10:24
- "Let each of you look not only to his own interests, but also to the interests of others." Philippians 2:4

Complaining—

- "Do everything without complaining or arguing." Philippians 2:14

Disobeying—

- "Children, obey your parents in the Lord, for this is right. 'Honor your father and mother' (this is the first commandment with a promise), 'that it may go well with you and that you may live long in the land.'" Ephesians 6:1-3

- "Rebellion is as bad as the sin of witchcraft, and stubbornness is as bad as worshiping idols." 1 Samuel 15:23

Fighting, Arguing—

- "Let us not become conceited, provoking one another, envying one another." Galatians 5:26
- "A soft answer turns away wrath, but a harsh word stirs up anger." Proverbs 15:1

Rude, impatient, or disrespectful speech—

- "Let no corrupting talk come out of your mouths, but only such as is good for building up, as fits the occasion, that it may give grace to those who hear." Ephesians 4:29
- "Let there be no filthiness nor foolish talk nor crude joking, which are out of place, but instead let there be thanksgiving." Ephesians 5:4
- "But I tell you that men will have to give account on the day of judgment for every

careless word they have spoken." Matthew 12:36

DISCUSSION QUESTIONS

Chapter One

Behavior. Character is Key.

1. Fill in the blank.
Consistent behaviors reveal character, and ______________ is the key to child training.

2. What are some ways that a lack of character will be evident in a child or teenager's life?

3. What extra problems will adults and teenagers who lack godly character face?

4. What are some of the blessings of raising a child with godly character?

5. Read the "Godly Character Traits" list on pages 75-78. Write down the verse that stood out to you the most.

6. How can you improve as a mother based on the verse you wrote down in the previous question?

Chapter Two

Loves: Connecting with your children.

1. What are four ways to connect with your child?

   1)
   2)
   3)
   4)

2. What specific things do you do as a mother to connect with your children?

3. Is there anything you do that you don't need to be doing (internet forums, cooking elaborate meals, talking on the phone) that predisposes you to getting irritated with your children more easily? How can you cut down on those things so your focus can be on your children?

4. How do you view your kids? Is life better when they are at the babysitters? Are they an interruption or the joy and delight of your day?

5. How can you improve as a mother based on what you read in this chapter?

Chapter Three

Encourages. Teaches.

1. What are some of your goals for your children?

2. How can you make sure you accomplish those goals as a mother?

3. Are you actively working toward the salvation and sanctification of your children by the conversations you have with them?

4. Read Luke 6:40. When a person is fully trained, who will that person be like?

5. Who are the trainers and teachers of your children? Will you be happy if your children turn out to be just like their teachers?

6. How can you improve as a mother based on what you read in this chapter?

Chapter Four

Safeguard.

1. Fill in the blanks.

Proverbs 29:15 "The ______ and ___________ give wisdom, but a child left to himself brings ___________ to his mother."

2. Fill in the blanks.

Proverbs 13:20 "Whoever walks with the wise becomes wise, but the companion of fools will ______________ __________."

3. Are you willing to make sacrifices if those sacrifices will save your children from being unnecessarily influenced by the world?

4. How can you improve as a mother based on what you read in this chapter?

Chapter Five

Set an Example.

1. What character trait would you like to see your children improve? How can you improve in this area first to set the right example?

2. Whose behavior are your children going to reflect?

3. Do you see any negative behaviors in your children that they may be picking up from you? What can you do to change?

4. Are there ways you could do a better job of modeling godly character for your children?

5. Are there any specific ways you could improve how you treat or react to your children?

6. How can you improve as a mother based on what you read in this chapter and on the "Godly Character Traits" list?

Chapter Six

Disciplines. Establishing Rules.

1. How does disciplining your children teach them that sin is very serious?

2. Read the "Sinful Behaviors" list in the Resources at the back of this book. Have you been overlooking any of these sins in your children?

3. What are some of your personal rules for your kids that have helped you maintain order in your house? What are some of your household rules that have really helped you and/or your family?

4. What are some activities your children could do or responsibilities you could assign them to better occupy your their time so they are too busy to argue or fight?

5. Can you expect your child to be consistent with obedience if you are not consistent with discipline?

6. Why is it wrong to seek your child's approval? See Galatians 1:10.

7. How can you improve as a mother based on what you read in this chapter?

ABOUT THE AUTHOR

Katie Hoffman lives in Dallas, Texas with her husband Todd and their 3 children. She speaks to women nationwide about the truths in God's Word—and loves it!

Please feel free to contact her with any questions or comments you may have. She'd love to hear from you!

katie@katiehoffman.org
www.katiehoffman.org